Original title:
The Soft Touch of Silk

Copyright © 2025 Creative Arts Management OÜ
All rights reserved.

Author: Theodore Sinclair
ISBN HARDBACK: 978-1-80586-013-6
ISBN PAPERBACK: 978-1-80586-485-1

Interlaced in Graceful Harmony

In a world where fabrics dance,
Threads embrace with just a chance.
A cat slips on a shiny sheet,
And lands with grace—not so discreet.

Colors clash, yet hearts agree,
Stitches giggle, wild and free.
A tie-dyed shirt becomes a cape,
As fashion's folly takes its shape.

Flutters of Silk and Time

A dapper owl in satin vest,
Claims he's looking simply best.
Pigeons strut in ruffled pride,
Feathers fluff, as down they glide.

A scarf takes flight upon the breeze,
Entangled in the branches, trees.
It whispers jokes, a fabric tease,
And ducks all quack in gleeful wheeze.

Hues of Velveted Memories

A patchwork quilt of thoughts so bright,
Stitched with laughter, no need for fright.
Each little square a tale to tell,
Of snags and mishaps, fits so well.

A tapestry where dreams align,
A zipper stuck, oh, isn't that fine?
Old socks chat in muted hues,
As laughter echoes in worn-out shoes.

Daring Dreams in Fabric Form

In a wardrobe where secrets loom,
A superhero costume makes room.
Badges of courage sewn with glee,
All designed for a bold cup of tea.

A cape that flops, a mask askew,
Who knew heroics could smell like stew?
Daring dreams with a comedic twist,
In shiny pants, you can't resist!

Serene Charms of Fabric

In a closet full of fluff,
Hiding treasures, oh so tough.
I reached for something quite divine,
A rogue sock slipped, it crossed the line.

I laughed and spun, what a sight,
Dancing threads, oh, what delight!
The button's range, a game of chance,
My clothes just want to steal the dance.

Velvet Night

Under stars, I chose my dress,
Soft and smooth, but what a mess!
A cat climbed up, I lost my cool,
Now it's more a furry golden rule.

With ruffles swirling, I made a spin,
The fabric whispered, 'Let's begin!'
But as I twirled, I tripped and fell,
Turns out, evening wear loves to rebel.

Silken Day

In sunlight's grace, I donned my gear,
A silky shirt, oh what a cheer!
But then a breeze, and my hair took flight,
Now I'm just a walking kite!

With laughter shared over morning brew,
I spilled my toast, oh what a view!
The breadcrumbs cling like a fashion trend,
I guess this day just needs a mend.

Cascade of Delicate Textures

In my closet, layers piled high,
One hasty choice made me sigh.
I looked like a cake, oh what a treat,
But all my friends just felt the heat.

With frills and lace, I hit the street,
The world gazed on my shimmering feat.
Yet as I turned, my scarf got stuck,
Now I'm the queen of textile luck!

Moonlit Drapes of Dusk

A stroll beneath the silver glow,
In flowing cloth, I put on a show.
But as I swayed, I nearly tripped,
The moon just chuckled, 'What a script!'

With every step, I left a trace,
Of tangled threads in a wild chase.
Yet laughter echoed, what a blast,
Even moonlight knows how to cast!

Gossamer Paths of Laughter

In the garden of giggles, we flit,
Dancing like shadows, not one bit lit.
A breeze knocks the knickers off a bush,
As we run from the tickle of a tiny mush.

Fabric of joy woven into times,
Swirling in whispers, making silly rhymes.
We trip on the threads that hold our cheer,
Wrapped in the colors of laughter so dear.

A Symphony of Silken Hues.

Bright colors clash like a puppy parade,
Socks and shorts—oh, what a charade!
The cat joins in, with a glimmering bow,
As we waltz through the mess, smiling somehow.

Each twist of the fabric's a jest, indeed,
A patchwork of giggles, like a joyful seed.
We slip and we slide, a fashion faux pas,
Yet every mishap gets us an applause.

Whispers of Midnight Fabric

Under the stars, in pajamas so bright,
We plot in whispers, what a strange sight!
The lamp's gentle glow reveals a caper,
As we craft our tales under quilted paper.

With threads of mischief softer than dreams,
Laughter erupts like raucous moonbeams.
A dance with the shadows, we prance and we sway,
In our midnight attire, we steal the day.

Caress of Gossamer Threads

The breeze tickles toes, it's quite a delight,
As we leap on the lawn in the pale moonlight.
With a flick of our robes, oh, what a sight!
We tumble and giggle, oh, such a fright!

These threads intertwine, like our silly mess,
Creating a tapestry of humorous stress.
With every ridiculous fumble and spin,
We wear our blunders like a cheeky win!

Dances of Delicate Fabrics

A curtain twirls and flops, it seems,
Much like my cat chasing her dreams.
With every flutter, a giggle escapes,
As granny's old quilt slips and scrapes.

In the breeze, it prances and sways,
Tickling toes in the sill of sun's rays.
The couch cushions join in the show,
Throwing a dance party, oh what a glow!

A Tapestry of Gentle Touches

Once a tablecloth had dreams high,
Of being a superhero, oh me, oh my!
But it ended up stained with spaghetti sauce,
Now part-time table, it bathes in its loss.

Napkins flap like birds on the fly,
Dodging forks from dinner, oh my, oh my!
They giggle and chatter with every fold,
Spilling secrets of dinner, all uncontrolled!

Floating on Feathered Whispers

A pillow floats, plush and round,
Whispers of dreams all around.
With each head bump, it erupts in jests,
'This is my spot!' it firmly protests.

Feathers burst forth in wild delight,
As bedtime battles commence each night.
The duvet joins in, a then, 'Oh dear!'
As laughter erupts, soft snickers we hear.

Veils of Light and Shadow

A curtain peeks through the breeze,
Covering the light with crafty degrees.
A dance of shadows plays on the wall,
Silly shapes morphing, having a ball.

Drapes that swing like on a pogo stick,
Making the world giggle, oh what a trick!
They poke out faces, one after the next,
A magic show where nothing makes sense!

Embraced by Dreamy Tapestries

When I trip on this fabric, oh my, what a sight,
My legs in a dance, a hilarious plight.
Like a clown on a pogo, I bounce to and fro,
This playful mishap, my entrance to show.

Threads whisper secrets, tickle my chin,
A blend of confusion, laughter begins.
Wrapped in bright colors, I twirl and I sway,
After a tumble, I'm lost in the fray.

Emotions Wrapped in Lush Layers

A scarf thrown on carelessly, what a surprise,
It dangles like spaghetti from my two wide eyes.
Feeling all fancy, yet a comedic charm,
Who knew dressing up could lead to alarm?

Cloaked in fine fibers, I prance like a queen,
But trip on my hem—oh, what a scene!
With each little dance, I flutter and glide,
In this silky embrace, I giggle and slide.

Caressing the Edge of Enchantment

Fluffy and cuddly, this costume divine,
But when I bend down, oh no—it's all mine!
Caught in a whirl, round and round like a top,
A shirt full of laughs that just won't stop.

Draped like a goddess, I feel oh so grand,
But step on my gown, and it's slapstick, unplanned.
The mirror's laughing back—what's this silly jig?
In layers of luxe, I dance like a pig.

Layered Love in Silken Caress

Wearing my ruffles, I'm queen of the ball,
But hey, is that static? I'm stuck on the wall!
With each little move, I'm pulling a prank,
Turning my outfit into a floaty flanked tank.

Twirling with vigor, I dizzy and spin,
In this fabric's embrace, a giggle sneaks in.
Like jellybeans mixing in a giant stew,
My wardrobe's a circus, and I'm the zoo crew.

Lush Embrace of Midnight Hues

In the closet, secrets hide,
A rainbow lounge, fabric's pride.
Plush and sassy, all in line,
A fabric party, oh so fine.

Worn by cats who think they're grand,
Prancing through the living land.
But wait! The curtains start to sway,
Caught the feline in mid-play!

Oh what fun, a fabric dance,
A splash of mischief, a daring prance.
The dog stands watch, it's quite a show,
As chaos reigns in textile flow.

Midnight hues and plenty of flair,
How can one not stop and stare?
A comedy of threads so spry,
Next on stage, the bunny will fly!

Fluttering Afterglow of Satin

Once, a kite made of sheer bliss,
Caught a breeze, oh what a miss!
It whispered tales with gentle laugh,
But crashed into the garden path!

With petals soft, it made a bed,
Said the ladybug, 'No need for dread!'
I wrapped myself in golden threads,
Marveled at my fancy spreads.

An impromptu party, flit and spin,
Blowing kisses in the din.
Who knew that fabric could throw a bash,
A satin soirée, a whimsical clash?

As the sun set with a playful grin,
The worms in suits joined right in.
With laughter that could lift the sky,
What a sight, oh my, oh my!

Ephemeral Drapes of Beauty

Once I stole a roll of lace,
Wrapped it round my neighbor's face.
He thought it was a grand disguise,
A film star in a fabric prize.

The curtains twirled with flair and glee,
Caught the laughter of our spree.
My dog said, 'I need a silly hat,'
So we dressed him up like that!

Ruffles here and ruffles there,
Lace like clouds, a flowing layer.
Elves were twirling in surprise,
Who knew such mischief would arise?

A flash of color, wild and free,
Drapes of dreams, oh please do see.
They tease the wind, oh what a sight,
Dancing under the stars so bright!

The Grace of Woven Clouds

Clouds in my closet hold contests,
Which fabric floats and looks the best?
Velvet candidates keen to impress,
While corduroy makes quite a mess!

A cotton parade, colorful song,
Swirling through air, oh, so strong!
"Vote for me!" the spills all plead,
But who will win this fabric creed?

With a wink, I tossed a scarf,
A twirl of joy—a fluffy serf!
Plumes of laughter filled the air,
No fabric rival could compare.

So I wear them, hat on side,
With every spin, my pride is wide.
The woven clouds, oh what a team,
Making mundane life a dream!

Sensuous Embrace of Weave

A scarf flew by, oh what a sight,
It wrapped a cat, gave quite a fright.
The feline leapt, all fur and flair,
Draped in threads, it danced in air.

In a cupboard high, a blouse took flight,
It tickled noses, oh what delight!
A twist, a turn, it sought some fun,
In the fashion race, it surely won.

A curtain swayed, with a graceful leap,
It caught the wind, played hide and seek.
Neighbors laughed from their viewing spots,
As fabric morphed into funny knots.

Fine threads of joy, all tangled too,
Creating giggles, and a funny view.
In this textile realm, where laughter reigns,
The soft entanglement brings joy, not pains.

A Dance of Fine Fibers

Two socks teamed up for a wild jig,
Spinning round with a cheeky gig.
One slipped and fell, oh what a show,
The laundry basket cheered, 'Go, go, go!'

A belt debated with a pair of jeans,
"Should I be tight or float like dreams?"
They tangoed softly in the closet space,
A fashion duel, a lively race.

While scarves performed a lovely waltz,
One tripped on lace, began to halt.
With every twist, they aimed to please,
Oh how they teased, with elegant ease.

In their dance of silk, so bold and bright,
Laughter echoed through the fashionable night.
These playful fibers spun tales so grand,
Bringing joy with every twirling strand.

Luminous Pleats of Bliss

A dress spun round in a dazzling dash,
Flipping pleats like a colorful splash.
It caught a breeze and flew with glee,
Knocking over a vase—oh dear me!

The trousers joked with a shirt quite fine,
"Together we look like we're ready to shine!"
But they tangled up in a messy heap,
They laughed it off, "We're cool and cheap!"

In a world of colors, they staged a play,
Pants and skirts in a bright ballet.
With every leap of fabric flair,
They filled the air with laughter rare.

Though the collar slipped off the dressy coat,
No one cared, it just meant some more fun wrote.
In a circus of fabric, they waved and twirled,
A riot of joy in a textile world.

Veils of Tenderness

A sheer veil floated, all soft and sweet,
It tickled a nose and made it retreat.
Oh the battle of sneezes it led to fame,
In the world of fabrics, it found its game.

A handkerchief slid down, took a chance,
It joined the fray in a fabric dance.
With every flutter, it fanned up the room,
Spreading giggles and a hint of perfume.

The tablecloth rolled, with a chuckle and sway,
It draped a chair, like it knew the way.
A family gathered, all tucked in tight,
And the fabric whispered, "Isn't this right?"

With each fold and pleat, a story untold,
In the land of textiles, laughter unfolds.
From delicate threads, a tapestry bright,
Brings humor and joy, a splendid sight.

Delicate Hues of Embracing Light

A butterfly danced on my nose,
It tickled my thoughts, oh, what a pose!
I giggled out loud, my coffee did spill,
Chasing that flutter, I lost all my chill.

The sun peeked in with a cheeky grin,
Casting soft colors, where does it begin?
My shirt unmatched, but who really cares?
With hues of chaos, life's fun, I declare!

Soft Glint of Morning Dew

Woke up this morning, the grass had a shine,
Fell on my backside, what a slippery line!
Those droplets were giggling, a prankster's affair,
Now I'm a puddle, with dew in my hair.

The plants were all laughing, what a sight to see,
Each blade a comedian, tickling me.
I joined in the chuckles, oh, what a view,
Nature's own mirror—who needs a shampoo?

Enfolded in Velvet Wishes

Wrapped in a blanket, like a burrito,
Dreams of sweet snacks, yes, I'm the star of the show.
But with one little sneeze, oh, what a disaster,
Chips flew like confetti, laughter came faster!

Velvet wishes whisper tales of delight,
But crumbs on my shirt? A common sight!
Each wish that I make, to be snack-proof instead,
Turns out to be jokes, I'm well-fed, well-read.

Blissful Layers of Memory

In layers of laughter, we build up our days,
Falling like pancakes, in syrupy haze.
Each flip a new story, as grand as can be,
Who knew breakfast could bring such glee?

Grandma's old tales, like soft, fluffy clouds,
Wrap us in warmth, her wisdom so loud.
But watch out for spice, it might tickle your nose,
Randomly sneezing? Now that's how it goes!

Gentle Glimmers of Grace

In a closet hid a rogue,
With laces tied in knots,
Every evening turned a joke,
As I danced with my own thoughts.

Feathers tickle on my face,
A scarf flutters with glee,
Chased by a cat, what a race,
My laughter brings them to me.

In grandmas purse, do not look,
Lurks a silky, shiny prize,
Whispers of a fashion book,
Of strutting cats with high-class ties.

At parties, I slide and swoosh,
A trail of giggles they see,
With each move, I try to push,
The limits of my clumsy spree.

Chiffon Breezes at Twilight

A chiffon ghost floats on by,
It's fluttering like it's alive,
The neighbors blink and ask why,
I'm wearing Granny's old jive.

In the moonlight, it reveals,
A dance of shadows, quite profound,
But tripped over my own heels,
Now I'm free, flapping around.

When the breeze caught it just right,
I became a kite on a thrill,
My friends laughed, it was delight,
As I soared a bit up the hill.

At twilight, the chaos roams,
With laughter and a fabric chase,
Expecting it to find new homes,
It flaps and flutters with grace.

Hidden Petals in Softness

A dress hides out like a spy,
Petals in pockets, they peek,
I waddle, no need to fly,
Every step brings out a squeak.

Flowing fabric, wild and bright,
Sneaking snacks in the seams,
At the picnic, oh what a sight,
My lap is a treasure of dreams.

Frolicking with friends, a breeze,
Causing a ruckus, oh dear me,
Petals swirl, each laugh brings ease,
Turning this day into glee.

Like a magician at play,
My dress can make a spice blend,
Keep your quirks at bay,
Next time, I just won't pretend.

Caressing Shadows of Soft Fabric

Fabric drapes across the floor,
Like a well-trained puppy dog,
Trying to find a cozy core,
I trip, it laughs, and I log.

In a game of hide and seek,
It whispers secrets in my ear,
With a soft and silly cheek,
As my friends approach, I fear.

A ghostly sheet throws off the light,
Like it owns the room, indeed,
Twists me as I try to fight,
Now I stumble, oh, what a speed!

These shadows dance, they tease my mind,
As I tumble, wiggle, and roll,
In this fabric, joy I find,
Even if it swallows me whole.

Enigmatic Layers of Whispered Love

In a world where cotton reigns supreme,
Silk tiptoes in to join the dream.
It sneezes at the thought of fraying,
Yet offers charms that leave you swaying.

Beneath the layer, secrets play,
A mishap leads to quite the fray.
A slip, a slide, a laugh erupts,
Fashion faux pas, but who disrupts?

With every touch, a giggle grows,
And tangled threads, oh how it shows!
Whispers shared beneath the stars,
Mixed with laughter, life's bizarre.

Oh love, your fabric's quite the tease,
It rolls me up like fallen leaves.
Wrapped in layers, what a sight,
In silky chaos, hearts take flight!

Dreams Adrift on Silken Boats

In rivers where the satin flows,
Dreams set sail with capsize woes.
They giggle as they drift afar,
Chasing cheese and shooting stars.

A boat made soft as clouds above,
With oars that whisper tales of love.
But wait, what's this? A snaggy mess,
A means to chase a silk-pressed dress!

The captain's hat, a floppy dream,
Sails made of ice cream, or so it seems.
With laughter echoing through the night,
On silken waves, we sail delight!

So join the ride and catch some glee,
On boats of silk, we'll drift carefree.
With drowsy waves and a silly cheer,
Life's a party, let's steer clear!

Memories Stitched in Softness

In the attic, fabrics lay,
Memories stitched in disarray.
Each thread a giggle, a twist of fate,
Wrapped in whispers, oh what a state!

A quilt of laughter worn with pride,
While a cat dreams and tries to hide.
Paws entangled in colors bright,
An epic battle, a silly sight!

With every fold, a chuckle's found,
Softness leaps, jumping all around.
Like childhood games in sunlight's glow,
Those stitched-up tales, we still hold close.

In patches worn, we see the fun,
Life's quilted moments, never done.
So snag a thread, and let's unwind,
To softer days, we will rewind!

The Allure of Whispering Threads

In the closet, secrets loom,
Whispered threads in a fabric tomb.
A snip, a clip, oh what a bluff,
Cotton's sturdy, but silk is tough!

They tangle and play, an agile dance,
Silken threads are full of chance.
With every twirl and playful tease,
We find ourselves brought to our knees!

Chasing fibers like a game of chase,
A stubborn knot we can't erase.
But laughter fills the fabric air,
In this madness, nothing can compare!

So weave your jokes and share the fun,
For threads of joy, they weigh a ton.
In whispers soft, we find our groove,
With each bright twist, our spirits move!

Laced with Subtle Caress

A fabric so fine, it dances with flair,
Creeping around corners with nary a care.
It tickles my toes, oh such a delight,
I trip over threads in the middle of night.

My cat treats it like a plushy arcade,
Pouncing and prancing, a soft little parade.
He finds it amusing to claw at my side,
While I'm trying to nap; oh, it's quite a ride!

A slip and a slide, oh what a sight,
It's draping my snacks; it's a curious plight.
As I munch on my chips, the fabric takes flight,
It's a snack-stealing ghost in the pale moonlight!

So here's to the fabric that wraps me in glee,
Each twist and each turn's a new comedy.
For in life's little moments, we laugh and we play,
With threads that surprise us in fun, silly ways.

A Symphony of Sighs and Textiles

Patterns that giggle with a rustle and shake,
Inviting my friends for a wild fabric break.
We twirl in the room, a textile ballet,
Each spin feels like laughter, come join in the fray!

My shirt has a personality—such a tease,
It makes fun of my dance moves with utter ease.
With generous flair, it flaps all around,
Making it clear I'm the joke of the town!

The bedspread grins as I dive into bed,
With surfaces whispering jokes in my head.
It steals all my dreams for a spacious reprieve,
Got me bouncing in laughter—who could believe?

Yet as I lay down, exhausted from play,
The comforting fabric urges me to stay.
It's soft and it's quirky, like a snug teddy bear,
Bringing giggles and sighs to the weary night air.

Silk Symphony in the Moonlight

In moonlight's embrace, a shimmer so sly,
Draped over good friends, we just can't deny.
We wear our shimmers like a playful parade,
We're fittingly clad in this nightly charade!

With laughter a'pinging, the fabric takes flight,
Every twist and a jingle, a silly delight.
I trip on a fringe, they dissolve in a fit,
As we giggle and cackle at every little bit.

The curtains are dancing, waltzing away,
They beckon with softness to come out and play.
A tug here, a tug there, they flow like a stream,
I'm tangled in moments more funny than dreams!

So here's to the evening, to fabrics and fun,
A silky escapade under the moon and sun.
In every soft whisper, a comic surprise,
Where laughter envelops, and joy never dies.

Murmurs of Genteel Fabrics

A wispy affair, with a nudge and a laugh,
Dressed like a peacock, oh my, what a path!
The couplings of textiles form giggling streets,
Where taffeta winks and the satin competes.

With swirls of confusion, we dance past the mirror,
"Do we look ridiculous?" it asks with a sliver.
"Oh splendid, it seems, we might have gone wild,
Yet in our bright clashing, we're simply beguiled!"

The couch made of velvet teases my style,
"Here, try a flip, love—I'm quite worth a while!"
But landing composed is a hilarious scrap,
As I clunk and I tumble in this zen-like nap.

So let's toast to the fabrics that sing with delight,
Whispering secrets beneath the soft night.
In life's quirky theater, they surely take part,
Tickling our fancies, and warming our heart.

The Lullaby of Woven Nights

In dreams, I glide on fabric threads,
Where laughter dances, and mischief spreads.
The cat in pajamas, quite a sight,
Chasing shadows in the dim moonlight.

Whispers of comfort in every seam,
Tickling my toes, oh what a dream!
A blanket fort that swallows all,
Where the pillows hold a midnight ball.

The sheets are singing a silly tune,
Making me giggle beneath the moon.
Naps are for bears, no room for rest,
Nighttime hijinks are always the best!

As I bounce like a springy bed,
With giggles echoing overhead.
The stars peek in through the fabric's grace,
Join the fun in this cozy space!

Tender Strokes of Timeless Fabric

A fancy dress with frills galore,
Twirls and swirls on the dance floor.
I bumble in a dapper suit,
But tripping's all I seem to loot.

Socks mismatched, a daring feat,
A fashion faux pas, oh what a treat!
But the crowd roars with such delight,
'Hey look! It's the jester of the night!'

The fabric hums with every stride,
While I stumble, fall, and then glide.
Who knew that fabric could be so funny?
Turned my mistake into sweet honey!

With a twinkle in my eye, I prance,
Dressed up in this ridiculous dance.
Every stitch holds a giggle tight,
In this fashion show of pure delight!

Sensuous Waves of Material Bliss

Rolling in fabric, I'm lost in fun,
Like a pile of laundry that just won't run.
Towels tangle in a fluffy heap,
I chuckle and laugh, this joy I'll keep.

The curtains flutter like they're alive,
Making funny faces, oh how they strive!
Yet one wrong step, and down I go,
In this wave of laughter, I'm stealing the show.

Shirts that sparkle like glittery dreams,
Tugging at me with their playful schemes.
Each fold and crease tells a joke,
Twisting my fate in a fabric cloak.

With every thread, I chase the cheer,
Waves of humor, I hold so dear.
In the sea of cloth, I dance and spin,
Where every snicker hides a grin!

Shimmer of Twilight Threads

Under the stars with twinkling light,
I wrap myself in colors bright.
My shirt's dancing like it lost its mind,
In this twilight glow, fun's intertwined.

The pants get all tangled, a wild knot,
As I shimmy and shake, oh what a plot!
Kooky patterns jumping in sight,
Fashion's a circus, pure delight!

Every shimmer's a chuckle, no doubt,
As I prance in my pajamas about.
Waving goodbye to the day's sweet toil,
With a giggle and a wink, I spin and coil.

Threads in the twilight, with laughter to share,
Each flick and flutter adds humor to the air.
In this woven wonderland, I'm free,
To dance like a dervish, just being me!

Hushed Radiance Beneath the Stars

Under a blanket of cosmic glow,
A cat wore a tie, quite the show!
With every pounce and fuzzy leap,
He charmed the starlight, dreams to keep.

Hiccups of laughter, whispers so light,
The moon snickered softly, oh what a sight!
Slippers in stripes danced on their own,
While marshmallow clouds giggled, full-blown.

Balloons tied to old trees in haste,
Each floaty giggle, a pixel of grace.
A tumble of fabrics, chaos galore,
Under the starlit, they rolled on the floor.

Timeless Comfort in Silken Skins

In a grand ball, a penguin wore lace,
Trying to waddle, with elegance and grace.
A bear in a bowtie, who thought he could dance,
Tripped over his paws, what a clumsy romance!

Silk worms conspired, they knitted a spree,
Stitches of laughter, oh where could it be?
Wrapping the forest in taffeta dreams,
While the trees laughed out loud, or so it seems.

Chasing the curtains, a kitten so spry,
Tripped on a thread, oh me, oh my!
Laughter erupted in a whirlwind of twirls,
As the night wore its laughter, adorned with swirls.

The Serene Dance of Fabric and Heart

A gnome in a dress, his hat tilted askew,
Swayed to the music, awfully blue.
With every spin, laughter took flight,
His feet tangled up, quite the funny sight!

Fish in a tux, with a dance quite bizarre,
They twirled and they splashed, a scaly avatar!
"Is this the right rhythm?" they gasped with glee,
As they flopped on the waves, a sea symphony.

Turtles donned scarves, they sashayed in delight,
With twinkle-toed hops, they danced through the night.
In this playful story, fabric and mirth,
A tapestry woven, of joy and worth.

Moonlit Threads of Rich Emotions

Under the glow of the night,
Strings of laughter intertwine.
Fabrics dance in a playful fight,
Emotions spin like fine vintage wine.

Jokes woven into every seam,
A patchwork quilt of glee.
With every thread, we chase a dream,
Tickling fancy, a jubilee!

Eyelashes flutter, mischief in air,
Giggling like kids at play.
Satin slips and sneaky dare,
Each stitch calls for a fray.

In this tapestry, we find our delight,
Crafted with humor's sweet charm.
Chasing shadows until the light,
In cozy warmth, we're safe from harm.

Weaving Whispers of Affection

Threads of banter weave us tight,
Laughter wraps like a warm embrace.
Chasing each other day and night,
In this playful, silken space.

Beneath the fabric, secrets hide,
Giggling whispers, soft and warm.
Every touch a playful ride,
Comfort found, like a charm.

Ticklish moments make us twirl,
In our cozy, crafty nest.
Stringing together a joyous swirl,
Love's soft fabric, truly blessed.

In this weaving of silly dreams,
We find joy, like colors bright.
Patchwork laughter, bursting seams,
Crafted in giggles, pure delight.

Delicate Boundaries of Comfort

Between the layers, we gently tease,
Silken boundaries play a game.
Each poke and prod brings us to ease,
Wrapped in comfort, feeling no shame.

With every twist and playful bend,
We find laughter in the fray.
Cotton candy humor to send,
As silk drapes in a quirky way.

We tiptoe on this gentle line,
Balancing giggles on fine threads.
In this space, our hearts align,
Where tickles and warmth are widespread.

In a cocoon of warmth we stay,
Bordered by laughter and mirth.
With a wink and a quirky say,
Creating joy, a soft rebirth.

Floating Thoughts in Silken Realms

In a land where giggles sparkle bright,
Softly drifting on puffy clouds.
Thoughts float free, a whimsical flight,
Whispers giggle, enchanting crowds.

Satin skies above our heads,
With laughter sewn into the seams.
Playful tales where no one dreads,
Innocent laughter fuels our dreams.

Each thought like a feather, light and free,
Swaying gently on the breeze.
Ticklish wonders, glee decrees,
Softly wrapping thoughts with ease.

Among these realms, we drift and play,
Cocooned in joy, soft as a sigh.
Floating thoughts to brighten the day,
In this playful dance, we fly.

Shimmers of Satin Skies

In a world where feathers drum,
Everyone's dancing, what a hum!
Balloons fly high, pink and gray,
While squirrels join in, hip-hip-hooray!

Underneath the bright confetti,
A penguin slips, oh so unsteady.
With no care, he does a twirl,
Holding cupcakes, what a swirl!

Laughter bubbles, puffs of cheer,
The cat steals snacks, oh dear, oh dear!
Clumsy gnomes wobble in delight,
Tip-ponging off each other, what a sight!

As night drapes its velvet cloak,
A parrot croaks a silly joke.
In satin skies, the fun won't end,
With mischief and joy, around the bend!

Elysian Veils of Harmony

A panda prances, looking fine,
In sunglasses, sipping on brine.
Wrapped in laughter, clouds of fluff,
Squeaky ducks say, 'That's enough!'

Balloons get stuck in a tree,
While the raccoons do a spree.
Juggling donuts, lime and zest,
Who knew they could be so blessed?

Turtles race with a silly grin,
A dance-off starts, who will win?
With jellybeans line dancing too,
Beneath the stars, everyone's true!

The night ends with a grand parade,
With everyone dressed up, unafraid.
In veils of laughter, a joyful sight,
As stars wink down, oh what a night!

Breath of Luxurious Threads

A kitten wrapped, oh what a tease,
With tangled yarn, plotting with ease.
Rolling and tumbling, oh so spry,
Chasing sunbeams with a sly eye!

A hamster's wheel spins, fast as light,
While frogs jump high in pure delight.
With glittered shoes, they sway and glide,
Underneath a rainbow ride!

Teddy bears gossip, sipping tea,
'Did you hear? Oh, please, oh plea!'
Puppies parade in matching bows,
While everyone giggles at their toes!

As night creeps in with woolen hugs,
Sleepy heads find cozy rugs.
In luxurious threads, dreams take flight,
With laughter echoing, soft and bright!

Silken Serenades of the Heart

A giraffe struts in polka dots,
With a bow tie that simply plots!
He hums a tune, oh so refined,
While squirrels join, all intertwined.

The fish in the pond start to prance,
In swimwear, oh what a dance!
Boogie-woogie, splashes galore,
With frogs croaking, wanting more!

Under twinkling stars, a crew,
Dancing bunnies, what a view!
Spinning round in cacti hats,
Laughing hard, they chat like chats!

With a wink, the moon takes part,
Shining softly, a work of art.
In serenades, hearts play a part,
With joy and laughter, life's sweet start!

Patterns of Softest Reminiscence

Once I wore pajamas that did gleam,
Felt like a star in a silly dream.
They slipped off my body, oh what a sight,
Chasing them down, I quipped, "Not tonight!"

My cat claimed them as her new throne,
In her world, I was now overthrown.
With each soft pounce, she'd act rather proud,
I realized I wasn't in charge—oh loud!

Mom said they're cozy to wear, just right,
But they leave me tripping each day and night.
I laughed at the patterns, so bright and merry,
While running in circles, looking all hairy.

So here's to the fabric that slips and slides,
Bringing small mishaps and amusing rides.
If laughter can echo from threads that entwine,
Then truly, my wardrobe has humor divine!

The Art of Gentle Textures

I tried to craft a wrap, oh so fine,
But ended up wrapped like I've lost my mind.
Every tug turned into a colossal mess,
My couch became my well-dressed distress!

In the mirror I stood, a colorful sight,
With a robe of chaos, I lost my fight.
My dog gazed up, with a tilt of his head,
If fashion were farmed, I'd be plowed instead.

I asked for advice on the texture so light,
Got tips from a squirrel that seemed kinda bright.
She showed me her nest, all snug and tight,
I chuckled—fashion advice from a flighty bite!

Now I strut in the fabrics that tease and twirl,
Even if my style creates a good whirl.
Each thread weaves laughter through every attire,
A wardrobe of whimsy that never expires!

Tracing Edges of Tenderness

With every touch, I felt like a queen,
A squishy plush pillow, what could it mean?
Surely I'll conquer, with fabric so grand,
But there went my snack—it slipped from my hand!

I leaned on my couch as I munched on my chip,
It traveled right down, a slippery dip.
In a race with the cushions, a soft, crafty thief,
Who knew home could turn into a giggle relief?

I donned my best scarf, it flew with flair,
Till it entangled me in a cozy snare.
Friends laughed as they freed me with grains of cheer,
Matching a handbag, and all they could hear!

My life's an art of pink fluffed delight,
Where laughter and fabric twine through the night.
With edges so gentle, they soften the fall,
Making each tumble a joke for us all!

Echoes of Soft Connection

With fabric so fuzzy, hands reach out wide,
I swayed left and right, almost purled in pride.
"Who needs a hug when I've got this wrap?"
I winked at my friends, both snickers on tap.

They caught me slipping, my foot on the seam,
Fell head over heels—oh, what a dream!
I laughed on the floor, feeling soft and grand,
An echo of joy started spreading the land.

Fashion and folly, a match made of fun,
As patterns danced lightly—oh, how they run!
Just when I thought I'd perfected the style,
A feathered boa turned into a aisle!

In every mishap, a story will bloom,
Where laughter erupts from a wardrobe's room.
These gentle connections, bright and sublime,
Bring giggles and joy, prose wrapped in rhyme!

Whispers of Sateen

In a world where fabrics dance and swirl,
Cotton jeans just frown, they twirl.
I slipped on some satin, felt so grand,
But went for a jog and it slipped from my hand.

It shimmered and flashed like a shiny fish,
With every step, it granted a wish.
Caught in the breeze, it waved goodbye,
I chased it down, oh my, oh my!

Neighbors laughed, thought I was mad,
Running in circles, oh, how I had!
But in those moments, joy took flight,
With fabric so fancy, it felt just right.

Now every time I get dressed up fine,
I ponder the chase of that satin line.
Yet every giggle makes me feel chic,
In a world of cloth, adventure we seek.

Caress of Gossamer Dreams

In the closet hung a sheer delight,
A veil of whispers caught in my sight.
I donned it quickly, felt like a queen,
Stumbled down stairs, what a silly scene!

It floated like clouds, soft as can be,
Wrapped me in laughter, all eyes on me.
I spun like a record, round and around,
Only to fall, not making a sound.

The fabric still danced, it laughed, oh so bright,
While I lay there thinking, "Was that a kite?"
Oh the joys of light cloth, fickle and free,
What a lesson in grace, just look at me!

Now whenever I see that gossamer glow,
I giggle and think of my graceful show.
For life's a parade of fabric and fun,
And I'll keep twirling until I am done!

Silkbound Reverie

I dreamt of a party in a dress of bright thread,
With satin so fine, I was ready to spread.
But one wrong move, I slipped on a toy,
Landed face-first, can you hear the joy?

Friends peered down, all wearing a grin,
"Is that a new dance? Are you trying to win?"
I laughed and I rolled, so snug in my dress,
What had been elegance turned into a mess.

The silk formed a cocoon, I was caught unaware,
Like a worm on its way to a stylish affair.
Morning glories floated in colors so slick,
And all I could do was play parlor trick.

So here's to the fabric that keeps spirits high,
Even when you tumble or trip, oh my!
In this shimmery world, let laughter unfurl,
For silkbound reveries can turn into twirls.

Threads of Elegance

In a bustling room, a shimmer did gleam,
I thought I was classy, a true fashion dream.
But one hasty leap to greet my dear friend,
Out flew my top, what a twist to the end!

It caught the chandelier, a dazzling sight,
As I stood there chuckling, not feeling quite right.
"Just giving a show!" I shouted with glee,
While fancy threads spun in a wild jubilee.

A tug of a hem, oh what a delight,
Threads of elegance danced through the night.
Every thread laughed, they felt so alive,
As I turned my faux pas into a sweet jive.

And now my wardrobe is cotton and lace,
For I've learned the chaos can brighten the space.
In this world of fabric, I'll always find cheer,
With threads of elegance, nothing to fear!

Threads of Serenity Unspooled

In a world where stitches often break,
I found a fabric that made me shake.
It twirled me round with playful flair,
And whispered secrets in the air.

My cat, intrigued, danced near my feet,
Tangled in threads, oh what a feat!
She looked like a jester with a crown,
As I laughed and chased her around.

With every tug, the fabric sighed,
Like it was laughing, oh what a ride!
I wrapped it tight, then let it go,
And watched it flutter with a show.

So here's to fabrics that tease and play,
Turning a dull, mundane day.
For in each fold and every seam,
Lies a world that sparkles and gleams.

Satin Sorrows and Joyful Gleams

Oh satin dreams that slip away,
In the drawer, they want to stay.
I tried to wear you on my head,
But ended up in a knot instead!

My morning coffee spilled with glee,
As your sheen shone right off of me.
The barista laughed, my shirt did gleam,
It became a laughing, slippery theme.

I thought I'd dance in flowing grace,
But ended up in an awkward race.
My friends all watched with giddy cheer,
As I twisted, turned, and lost my rear!

Yet through the chaos, joy was found,
In every slip and goofy round.
So raise a glass, let's all redeem,
Our satin sorrows with a beam!

Breath of Textured Reverie

In realms where fabric plays the muse,
A cheeky touch gives me the blues.
I wrapped my dreams in cozy folds,
But found they were just a bit too bold.

With one swift move, I stretched and sighed,
Only to find my shirt had died.
It clung to me like a hug too tight,
In folds and creases, what a sight!

I reached for comfort, got a twist,
Envelope of fabric I just missed.
It laughed as I untangled woe,
Becoming a fashion faux pas show!

Yet every wrinkle told a tale,
Of adventures woven without fail.
So in this whimsical, fabric whirl,
I found the giggles made me twirl.

Glimpses of Ethereal Comfort

Ethereal threads that make me grin,
They drape and sway like a win-win spin.
I tried to waltz, but tripped on lace,
A friendly snicker in my face.

A scarf that flutters like a bird,
Wrapped 'round my neck with just a word.
It whispered softly, "Let's have fun!"
Yet left me hanging, now I run!

With every twist, my heart would race,
In fun-filled war with fabric's grace.
I'd pull and tug, it would protest,
A game of tag, a fabric jest.

But through the laughter, joy prevails,
As comfort wrapped me with itsails.
So come join in this playful spree,
Where fabric dances wild and free!

Warm Embrace of Dusk's Fabric

As evening creeps, the sill's awash,
With threads that shimmer, oh so posh.
A cat strolls by, with aplomb so grand,
In a cloak of clouds, there's laughter unplanned.

Whispers giggle on breezy nights,
As moths don gowns of satin lights.
They dance like dancers, twirling in space,
In their fancy get-ups, quite the faux pas grace.

Neighbors peek out, a curious sight,
Wondering about this gala so bright.
With every swish and every twirl,
They wonder who's hosting this fabric swirl!

Oh, twilight, how you throw a soirée,
With frilly frocks for night's ballet.
We'll toast to fashion, so oddly awry,
In the soft embrace where shadows fly.

The Touch of Twilight's Finery

At dusk, we wear the softest shades,
Like buttered toast, on sunny glades.
A dapper dog, with bowtie askew,
Struts on the lawn, as if he knew.

The trees don wraps, the leaves all twine,
In a velvet hug, both soft and fine.
Squirrels play dress-up, claim the last peach,
As if they're royalty, just out of reach.

A firefly, dressed in flickering chic,
Is the top model for the week.
With each little flash, it winks with flair,
As twilight giggles, fills the air.

Jokes are stitched in every breeze,
As laughter rustles through the trees.
A fabric of fun, in cozy hues,
In twilight's finery, we'll share our news.

Draped in a Warm Embrace

Draped in layers of dreamy dreams,
Where nothing's ever quite as it seems.
The neighbors argue, who wore it best,
While cats roll in fabric, no time for rest.

The sun dips low in a silky blur,
As cows parade in their fanciest fur.
They moo in style, while pigs prance around,
In ribbons and bows, they fit the sound.

Chicken fashion shows are all the rage,
In feathered gowns, they take the stage.
With beaks held high, and flapping wings,
Who knew barnyard life could be such things?

With each gentle breeze that brushes our face,
We twirl with giggles in fabric's embrace.
A wild parade of whimsical glee,
In this soft embrace, just you and me.

Beauty Folded in Feathery Grace

At opal hour, the world unfolds,
As stories of mischief soon are told.
The moon chuckles in a shy, soft light,
As doves flaunt feathers, oh what a sight!

In gowns of gossamer, hearts take flight,
With a wiggle and jiggle, they dance in delight.
Laughter erupts from a very wise owl,
Who claims it's stylish to hoot and howl!

Behold the hedgehog in a puffy blouse,
Searching for sparkle, and maybe a spouse.
With every prickly turn, it's still so grand,
A dapper little creature, in demand!

As twilight swirls in colors bright,
We share our tales, from evening to night.
In feathery grace, with joy in our hearts,
Life's funny fabric, oh how it imparts!

Elegance in Every Fiber

A fabric that glimmers, a breeze in disguise,
Threads full of whimsy, where laughter lies.
Wrap me in comfort, let giggles abound,
In fibers so funny, where joy can be found.

With every soft stroke, a tickle ignites,
Draped in delight, the day feels just right.
Unruly like cats, they leap and they dance,
In a world spun with laughter, who needs a romance?

Fabrics of laughter, let's twirl, let's play,
Come join in this riot of color today!
A cascade of chuckles, a giggly parade,
In threads of pure joy, let worries all fade.

With elegance woven through jokes in between,
Life's grand tapestry is the silliest scene.
Oh, to be wrapped in this joyful delight,
Where laughter and fabric make every night bright.

Silken Days and Starry Nights

Beneath shimmering skies, our saga unfolds,
Each thread tells a story, each wrinkle, it molds.
With a wink and a chuckle, we skip through the day,
In whimsical textures, our worries give way.

Nighttime arrives with a playful embrace,
Stargazing in comfort, our own special place.
Sailing through dreams on a sailboat of glee,
With laughter as our compass, come wander with me.

Slumber in silks spun from giggles and cheer,
Who knew bedtime magic could be this sincere?
Tickles from shadows, the moon shines so bright,
In this, our fairytale, we dance through the night.

With dawn breaking softly, the adventure resumes,
In this world of enchantment, where silliness blooms.
So wrap up in laughter and skip through the sun,
In days filled with joy, we've only begun!

Velvet Dreams and Sensuous Streams

Dive into softness, where silliness beckons,
In flowing rich velvet, a giggle's affection.
Swooshing and swishing, it sings in delight,
Velvet or laughter, which tickles more right?

A waltz with the fabric, we dance through the day,
Our joy uncontained, like a parade in May.
With colors so bold, and patterns so wild,
Let's weave together, be free, like a child.

The fabric, it hugs with a grin and a wink,
Each fold a small joke, oh, what do you think?
In cushy companions, both silly and grand,
We'll twirl to the rhythm of laughter's own band.

So slumber in layers, wear joy on your sleeve,
In a world bright with whimsy, what else can you believe?

With dreams made of velvet and laughter, it seems,
We're wrapped in the essence of silliest dreams.

Chasing Clouds in Weavings

Chasing the clouds as they giggle and drift,
With threads of enchantment, it's quite the gift.
We weave our own tales, with smiles and threads,
Embroidery full of the joy that we spread.

A patchwork of moments, both silly and bright,
In layers of color, bringing delight.
With every new stitch, laughter dances so free,
In a quilt made for dreaming, come whisper with me.

Oh, the things that we find in the fabric we choose,
Not a worry in sight, just a line full of blues.
As we twirl in our fibers—what fun it would be,
To stitch up a rabble of whimsical glee!

So gather around, let's stitch up a tune,
In the dance of the threads, we'll be over the moon.
With each playful yarn and a twinkling eye,
Together in laughter, we'll soar to the sky.

Shattered Echoes of Tense Threads

In a closet lives a frayed old scarf,
It whispers secrets with a blush of half.
Worn once to parties with flair in our stride,
Now a fetch for dust bunnies, it tries to hide.

Once it danced at a fashion show,
Now tangled with socks, what a sad tableau!
It dreams of gliding, oh how it begs,
Instead, it's tied up with laundry's pegs.

Threads plot their escape, a wild, funny spree,
As they escape from shirts to live fancy and free.
They trip on the rug, oh what a sight,
In the land of the lost, they party all night.

With every step, they stretch and they laugh,
Thanking the dryer for their twisted path.
In this fabric world, where chaos prevails,
Who knew a wardrobe could tell such tales?

Emptiness Filled with Soft Weaves

In a fabric store, two bolts conspire,
"Let's prank that tailor," they giggle and tire.
They slip from the shelf, and roll on the floor,
"Oh the adventures, we simply need more!"

A dress made from cotton, oh what a calamity,
They spun in a whirl, in pure insanity.
The seamstress gasps, "What a bizarre twist!"
While fabrics laugh, they add to the list.

With thread and needle, they join in the mess,
Creating a gaffe that leaves quite the impress.
They fashion a couch—really just for a joke,
Where the cat perches proud, riding high on the poke.

These rolls of fabric love chaos and cheer,
Dancing on shelves with no sign of fear.
In a quiet room, they turn wild and brave,
Emptiness fills as they misbehave.

The Essence of Silk Unfolding

A rogue piece of satin darts through the door,
Saying, "Oh darling, life's such a bore!"
It takes to the town in an old shopping cart,
Dreaming of glamour, a true work of art.

But wheels get stuck in a puddle of glue,
And it's a parade—just me and you.
Satin's stuck in a shimmering plight,
Yet spins with laughter, what a hilarious sight!

It rolls under tables, slips past the crowd,
Daring any dresser to sing out loud.
With a wink to the fringe and a flourish it prances,
Offending the cotton, it spurs wild romances.

"Let's fray off the rules, let's break every norm,
Together we'll rise, in a fabulous storm!"
In a world draped in dreams, both soft and absurd,
Satin brings laughter, oh how it's stirred!

Blush of Petal and Fabric

A flowered dress just loves to sway,
Teasing the breeze, it dances all day.
"Oh, watch me twirl," it giggles with glee,
But trips on a petal—oh dear, oh fie!

In a burst of laughter, it lands on its seam,
A sudden bouquet—a thorny dream.
The daisies chuckle; they hide their delight,
As this petal princess takes flight in the night.

With ribbons in hair and mischief in mind,
She throws caution to winds, yet she'll always find,
A way to get tangled in the tall grass of fate,
For her style is a meadow, never too straight.

So laugh through the fabric of life without care,
For petals may flutter, but none can compare.
To the joy of a wardrobe bursting with charm,
Where each stitch, a giggle, keeps us all warm.

A Tapestry of Whispered Secrets

In a closet, chaos reigns,
Beneath the garments, laughter gains.
A sweater once lost, now found in style,
Its neck stretched wide, it couldn't help but smile.

A scarf once shy now plays the flirt,
Tickling noses, what a quirky alert!
Each thread a giggle, each seam a jest,
In this wardrobe, there's no room for rest.

Around the world, it starts to weave,
Whispers of fashion, they surely believe.
But slips and trips bring tales of mirth,
Fabric's mischief spreads joy on this Earth.

So let's not fret when fashion goes wild,
Join the fabric party, be bold, be styled!
In layers of laughter, we dance and sway,
As secrets in textiles come out to play.

Whispering Threads of Serenity

In the weaving of yarn, jokes intertwine,
A patchwork of laughter, oh so divine.
The tailor's pin pricks funny little spots,
He should've seen that coming—what a lot!

Five yards of fabric, a cat doth roam,
Sewing mishaps turn into its new home.
With every snip, a chuckle bursts out,
The thread now unravels, what's it all about?

Underneath the stitches, silliness brews,
A tale of a shirt made of bright rainbow hues.
It wore it too close, now it's feeling tight,
It dances through day, oh what a funny sight!

When ribbons collide in a playful embrace,
They twirl like dancers, winning the race.
So stitch together your joys with glee,
In whispered threads lies the key to be free.

Gentle Hues of Fabric Dreams

Colorful patches sing out in delight,
Crafty creations come to life at night.
A blanket that giggles at every fold,
Its warmth wraps you up, funny stories told.

Pastel clouds float, but don't be deceived,
They hide little monsters, quite hard to believe.
One turned a sock into a puppet so loud,
It danced in the kitchen, drawing a crowd.

Velvet curtains blush at the sun's gentle shine,
Yet they trip on their hem—oh, how they align!
They cover the windows, but what's their intent?
To keep in the laughter, now that's money well spent!

So gather your fabrics, bring them to play,
A quilt of giggles brightening your day.
In every fiber, a chuckle hums low,
From dreamy designs, watch the fun overflow.

Elegance Wrapped in Stillness

A gown that sways, pretending to be grand,
But trips over flat shoes, oops — wasn't planned!
It sighs with elegance, all poise and grace,
Yet takes a tumble, oh what a disgrace!

Lace bumps into jeans thinking it's a party,
Only to find the crowd feels quite hearty.
With threads in a tangle, it can't seem to choose,
Shall it dress up or just not give a snooze?

Ribbons argue about their hair-styling fate,
"Up in a bun?" "No way, that's too straight!"
So down they cascade for a fun messy look,
Who said elegance must follow the book?

And this fabric world, full of giggling seams,
Encourages whims and hilarious dreams.
With every misstep, new fun is around,
In elegance tangled, joy can be found.

Silken Embrace of the Evening

As night descends in fluffy wraps,
The world giggles in gentle gaps.
A cat on a sofa, a splash, a leap,
Soft landings mastered, no need for sleep.

The stars are dressed in smooth, fine lace,
While fireflies twirl in a silly race.
They bump into pillows, soft puffs of air,
Creating a ruckus without a care.

Laughter floats on silken beams,
Under moonlight, the world gleams.
A hug from a friend, warm as toast,
In this evening's fabric, we gently coast.

Every giggle, every grin,
In this embrace, let joy begin.
The night, a blanket, cozy and bright,
Wraps us up, laughing till the light.

Shadows Dressed in Luxurious Threads

Shadows pirouette in pretentious gowns,
Swaying and swirling, like circus clowns.
With every twirl, a mishap occurs,
As they trip on hems and overly large spurs.

The moon, a tailor, snickers with glee,
As shadows dance, so clumsily.
Fabric of laughter, bright and bold,
Whispers of secrets that never get old.

Fluffy companions join in the fun,
Chasing the shadows, they happily run.
In the wardrobe of night, all threads let loose,
Creating a comedy, no need for a truce.

With every stumble and graceful fall,
The night's a stage, the shadows enthrall.
Wrapped in humor, like a fanciful bed,
In luxurious layers, the antics spread.

Fabricated Dreams unbound

In a quilt of dreams, the silly abound,
Tangled in fabric, no hope to be found.
Whispers of fun float high and low,
As stitches unravel, laughter will flow.

Clouds made of cotton puff in the sky,
While stitching together a whimsical sigh.
Every thread tells a tale long and wide,
Of adventures that giggle, and truth that's fried.

Sailing on waves of this dreamy delight,
Pants made of laughter, a comical sight.
Frolicking in fields of bright, floppy yarn,
Chasing the mirth that the night has worn.

With every seam that's yanked and pulled,
A tapestry of joy, whimsically ruled.
In dreams, we're free, our hearts take flight,
Fabricated giggles paint the night right.

Gently Falling into Silken Layers

The morning drapes in a playful sheet,
As silken layers make daytime sweet.
Draped on the couch, a toast to the cheer,
Falling like feathers, nothing to fear.

Slippers that flutter, like socks with flair,
Chasing the coffee, everywhere, beware!
A dance to the kitchen, steps full of sass,
In this game of layers, we all let it pass.

Pancakes stack high, fluffy as dreams,
Toppled by laughter and syrupy beams.
Every bite brings a tickle of fun,
In a world where breakfast is never quite done.

As layers of laughter and joy intertwine,
We skip through the day, in silk we shine.
With playful heartbeats, silly and bright,
Let's tumble through life, oh what a sight!

www.ingramcontent.com/pod-product-compliance
Lightning Source LLC
Chambersburg PA
CBHW060130230426
43661CB00003B/373